PIONEERS
The Journey West

By Yannick Oney

World Discovery History Readers™

SCHOLASTIC INC.

New York • Toronto • London • Auckland • Sydney
Mexico City • New Delhi • Hong Kong • Buenos Aires

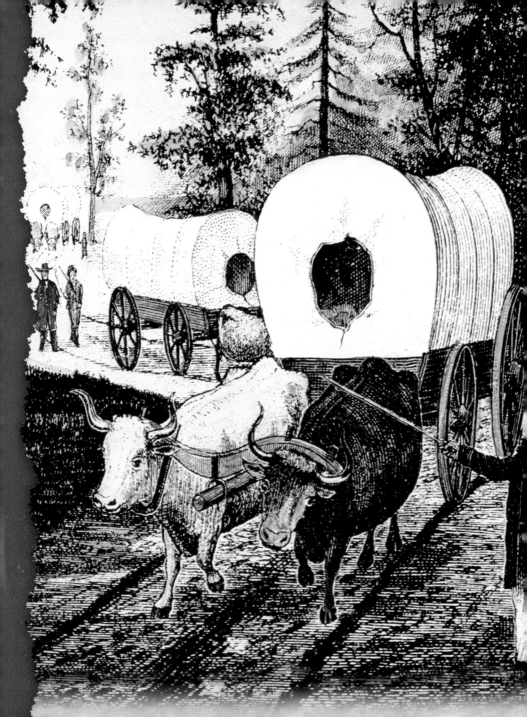

A wagon train traveling on the National Road in the
early 1800s. The National Road was first opened
by the United States government in 1818. Eventually,
it stretched all the way from Maryland to the
Mississippi River.

The Pioneers

Two hundred years ago, Americans knew of a mysterious land. It wasn't in a strange country. It was right in America. It was called the West. Americans hadn't yet traveled very far west. What was it like? Was it a big desert or covered in ice? Would the native people fight them or welcome them?

Then, slowly, mountain men and fur trappers started exploring the West. Soon, word spread that the West was beautiful. It was no longer mysterious. Americans decided to move there. At the time, there were no planes, trains, or cars. Traveling long distances was difficult. But it did not stop a huge wave of people, called **pioneers**, from leaving in covered wagons and heading west. This book is about these pioneers and the incredible journey they made.

Mountain man with his pack pony loaded with furs

Daniel Boone

CHAPTER 1

Who Were the Pioneers?

The first people to visit new places are called explorers. Explorers return home and tell the people there what they saw in the new places. People who decide to live in these new places are called pioneers.

Daniel Boone (1734–1820) was one of the country's first pioneers to head west. At the time, there were only thirteen colonies in America. They were all on the East Coast, and the land there was already settled and explored. Boone loved the wilderness. He also loved to discover new places. In 1775, he traveled west, away from the colonies. He made a trail from his home in Virginia to central Kentucky. The trail he blazed was called the Wilderness Trail.

Daniel Boone's first sight of Kentucky

Years later, when new pioneers headed west, they used Boone's Wilderness Trail. They loaded up wagons with food and supplies. Over time, pioneers decided to go farther west than they had ever gone before, all the way to land on the Pacific Coast called Oregon Country. To get there, they had to create their own trails.

Pioneers used six major trails to get to the West.

Legend
- Oregon Trail
- Santa Fe Trail
- Mormon Trail
- Gila River Trail
- California Trail
- Old Spanish Trail

Oregon Country

Salt Lake City

Independence

Sacramento

Pacific Coast

Santa Fe

Los Angeles

San Diego

Pacific Ocean

Between 1840 and 1890 more than 300,000 people packed up their belongings and journeyed 2,000 miles to the West. Their wagons were usually pulled by oxen

Homesteader family heading west with their belongings

or mules and traveled only about two miles an hour. They traveled so slowly that people could walk alongside the wagons and keep up. In 1841, the first group of families, the Bidwell–Bartleson Party, set out from Sapling Grove, Missouri, for the Far West. They were a group of sixty-nine men, five women, and ten children.

Pioneers move west

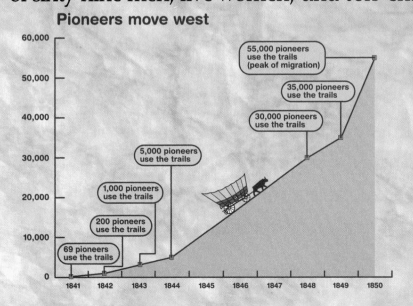

60,000

55,000 pioneers use the trails (peak of migration)

50,000

35,000 pioneers use the trails

40,000

30,000 pioneers use the trails

30,000

5,000 pioneers use the trails

1,000 pioneers use the trails

20,000

200 pioneers use the trails

10,000

69 pioneers use the trails

0

1841 1842 1843 1844 1845 1846 1847 1848 1849 1850

Homesteaders' cabins in the Red River Valley, North Dakota, 1800s

Pioneers were excited to start their trip. Farmers had dreamed of living on their own land. Now they could, in the West. They left in the spring. They wanted to avoid traveling during the winter when the weather was bad. When it came time to leave, farmers loaded supplies and plows and tools onto their wagons. Adults and children cried when they said good-bye to their friends and relatives. They might never see them again.

The pioneers knew they were moving to a beautiful place. They had read many magazines and newspapers that described the rich land in the West. Its forests had tall trees and its streams and rivers flowed strong.

Some covered wagons were also called prairie schooners.

Pioneers had many reasons to move west. Freed **slaves** called **Exodusters** went west to start a new life. They called the West "The Promised Land." In 1879, more than 50,000 freed slaves went to live in Kansas, Missouri, Indiana, and Illinois. In those states they could farm their own land.

People who belonged to the **Mormon religion** weren't welcome in the East. In 1847, Brigham Young, the president of the Mormon Church, helped the Mormons make their own trail west to Utah. There they could practice their religion freely.

Freed slaves moving into Kansas after the Civil War

Some people went west to dig for gold. If they were lucky, they might strike gold and become rich overnight. In 1848, gold was found in a small town called Sutter's Mill, California.

Sutter's Mill in California

Gold Fever struck in 1849! More than 30,000 people went west to look for gold. They were called **49ers**. 1849 was the beginning of the **California Gold Rush**.

Other people went west for jobs. **Cowboys** went to herd cattle on the open **plains**. **Lumberjacks** went to cut down trees. Doctors, lawyers, store owners, blacksmiths, and even criminals headed west.

Some went because there was more land to farm in the West. Others moved west simply for the adventure. Some thought life might be better there. The people who made the long journey all had one thing in common: They were all going to live in a new place. They were all pioneers.

11

Kit Carson, shown here with his horse Apache, was a famous guide.

CHAPTER 2

Hitting the Trail

A pioneer's first stop might have been Independence, Missouri. At the time, Independence was one of the most western towns in America. St. Joseph, Missouri, and Council Bluffs, Iowa, were other towns that pioneers went to when they started their journey west on the **Oregon Trail**. Pioneers joined together and made a **wagon train**. One wagon traveled behind the other. A mountain man or a trapper was hired to lead the way west.

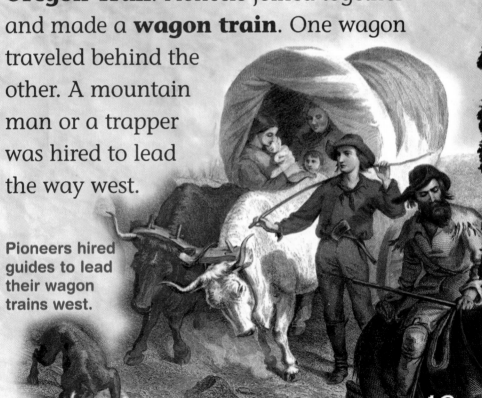

Pioneers hired guides to lead their wagon trains west.

As the wagons rolled west, children made friends. They played with one another as they walked the trail. "Watch out for rattlesnakes. Don't get lost," mothers said to their children. Sometimes children stopped to play hide-and-seek in the tall prairie grass. Or they went to watch the funny prairie dogs jumping in and out of holes in the ground. If the children got lost, the wagon train would not wait for them. Some children died left alone, and others were picked up by another wagon train following behind them. During the day, the wagon train had to keep moving.

Wagon trains left in early spring so they would get over the **Rocky Mountains** before the first heavy snow fell in late fall. If snow fell, the pioneers would be stuck in the mountains. They might freeze and die.

Prairie dogs were a common sight.

A pioneer boy and his dog

Wagon train in a snowstorm on the Great Plains

Being on a wagon train was like traveling with an entire town. There were a lot of people. Order had to be kept. Rules were made. Just like a town needs police to make sure people obey the law, wagon trains needed people to help make everyone obey the rules of the wagon train. Most wagon trains elected officers. Officers settled arguments and punished those who didn't obey the rules.

Pioneers woke up early, usually just before sunrise. Pioneers walked an average of fifteen miles a day and all the walking made everyone tired! Sometimes the animals stumbled along. If they suffered injuries on the trail, the pioneers had to care for them. If the pioneers got sick, they had to take care of one another.

Pioneers had to act as both doctors and veterinarians on the trail.

15

As the wagons continued to roll west, dust covered the pioneers' faces. There was dust in the bread they baked and dust on the salt pork they fried in a pan. Whenever they came to a place with a watering hole, they were never sure if the water was good or bad. Bad water carried diseases such as **cholera**. Many pioneers died from such diseases.

There was also a lot of sand on the trail. It rose up in strong westerly winds. Sand stung pioneers' eyes and made their eyelids swell. The sand was everywhere, but the nearest ocean was thousands of miles away. The sand came from the plains.

Men around a wagon train campfire at night

Pioneers trading with Native Americans

For safety at night, the wagons were pulled into a circle. The people and animals stayed in the middle of the circle.

Native people traded with the pioneers. The native people gave them moccasins and food in exchange for cloth and glass beads.

The Plains tribes, such as the Sioux, Cheyenne, and Pawnee, hunted buffalo. Huge herds of buffalo roamed the prairie. They looked like black clouds on the land. The buffalo could be dangerous. Loud noises scared them. When frightened, the buffalo sometimes started a **stampede**! Sometimes the pioneers would start a fire in the grass to keep the buffalo from running into the wagon train.

Native Americans hunting buffalo

It was the job of children to collect dry buffalo chips. These were the **droppings** from the buffalo.

American bison (buffalo)

Because there was not much wood on the prairie, the adults burned buffalo chips instead. Dry buffalo chips were flat like plates. Pioneer children sometimes tossed them back and forth and played a fun game of catch.

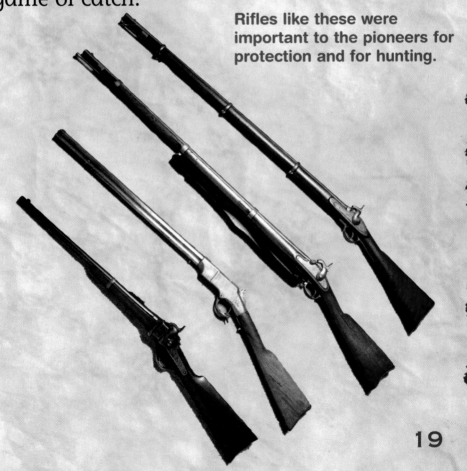

Rifles like these were important to the pioneers for protection and for hunting.

Sometimes after dinner or during lunch, the children on the wagon train had lessons. Mothers or fathers or other adults taught them. They studied math and learned to read from books called McGuffey's Readers.

The pioneers slept outside. When the night was clear, they could see hundreds of stars and hear wolves howling. When it rained, there was only enough room for a couple of people to sleep in the wagon. Parents and other adults usually slept inside the wagon, while children often slept under the wagon.

Family camped beside their covered wagons on the prairie

People hardly ever rode in the wagons. It was too bumpy. Stones and ruts in the trail made the ride too uncomfortable. When it rained hard, the trail became muddy. When the wagon leader gave the call for everyone to start rolling their wagons, it was hard to start moving. The wheels of the wagons got stuck in the mud. Women's and girls' skirts became so heavy with mud, they could barely walk.

Rivers rose in the rain and currents became very strong. Sometimes pioneers tied wagons together to get across the rivers. The wagons rolled through the shallow part of the rivers. But sometimes rough water made wagons tip over. Many pioneers drowned trying to cross rivers. Sometimes the pioneers used their wagons as rafts and the animals swam. Sometimes the pioneers even built log bridges so everyone could cross the rivers.

Covered wagon crossing a shallow river

Wagon train crossing the mountains

CHAPTER 3

Fort Laramie and Beyond

Walking beside a wagon day after day through the flat prairie could be boring and tiring. Everyone wished for a rest, a bath, and a chance to wash their dirty clothes. Just about when everyone thought they couldn't walk another step, the pioneers would arrive at Fort Laramie. They had reached Wyoming. After traveling for almost forty days, they could now rest for a few days at the Fort.

At Fort Laramie, pioneers bought new supplies and traded for goods with the native people. The pioneers had baths and washed their clothes. A day or so later, they got back on the Oregon Trail and headed for the Rocky Mountains.

Fort Laramie on the Oregon Trail

Independence Rock was one of the trail markers everyone looked out for so they knew how far they had come. When they got to it, some pioneers wrote their name on it with a paintbrush and tar. On July fourth, **Independence Day**, pioneers near Independence Rock gathered and ate a lot of good food. Someone played the fiddle and people danced. The children had sack races. Mothers and fathers talked about how good it would be to own their new land in Oregon. They talked about how they were free to go where they wanted. They liked knowing they could do things on their own without anyone's help. Years later, their thoughts about how to live life became known as the **Spirit of America**.

The pioneers needed to get past the Cascade Mountains before snow started falling.

The Columbia River

Some pioneers decided not to cross the Cascade Mountains. Instead they chose the dangerous trip of going down the raging Columbia River by raft or native canoe.

From Independence Rock, wagon trains would travel more than 1,000 miles to get to Barlow Road. Barlow Road took the wagon trains over the **Cascade Mountains**. Getting up the mountains wasn't easy. If the wagons were too heavy, pioneers had to lighten their load. Sometimes pulleys were used to lift the wagons and animals up the sides of mountains. The mountain passes were narrow. The trails twisted like a snake moving in the grass.

California emigrants' last camp on the plains before heading over the Rockies

CHAPTER 4

Trail's End

Finally, pioneers would come to where the trail split. People going to California turned off the Oregon Trail. They crossed through the harsh Nevada desert. Others continued the journey to Oregon Country.

Some people did not go that far. Before they reached the Rocky Mountains, they decided to settle on the prairie. There was little wood to build their houses, so settlers made their houses out of **sod**. It was cut into squares and used like bricks to build a house. The roof was made of sod as well, held up by wooden beams and branches. Doors were sometimes made of buffalo hides. People who lived in these houses were called "**soddies**".

Sod contains a lot of dirt, so sod houses were very dirty. Dirt even sprinkled down from the ceiling onto people's heads when they slept. Sometimes snakes would come down through the dirt roof and hang from the ceiling or drop to the floor.

Prairie farmers grew wheat, corn, barley, and other crops. Life on the prairie was hard. The climate was harsh. In winter, the temperature could reach forty degrees below zero. In summer, it could be a scorching 117 degrees. Blizzards blanketed the grassland with deep snow in winter, and tornadoes tore up the earth in summer. Heavy rains in spring flooded the rivers, and hail left holes in the ground. Grasshoppers ate their way through entire crops. Native peoples in the area weren't always friendly, either. They were angry that their land was being taken from them. Still, the farmers decided to live there. They began clearing the land and plowing it.

A pioneer family's sod house on the Kansas plains

In 1837, John Deere invented a plow with steel blades. Steel blades made it easier to plow the prairie land than the old cast-iron blades.

Sometimes it was lonely living on the prairie. Neighbors lived miles away from one another. On Sundays, children played together after church. There were dances and picnics, and once in a while the circus would come to town. Children went to school in a one-room schoolhouse. At home, the boys learned how to farm, plowing the tough prairie grass to make new fields. The boys learned how to run hay-cutting and **threshing machines** and how to build and repair houses. The girls learned how to make soap and candles and sew clothes. They learned how to cook and serve up big meals.

Sometimes pioneers traveling across the country thought they would never see Oregon Country. Then fall came, and the pioneers were now at the end of the trail in Willamette Valley. As they traveled, they started seeing deep green grass and tall trees everywhere they looked. The air was heavy with a soaking rain. Pioneers began to shout for joy—they had arrived at their new home!

Pioneers began to build houses using the tall trees of the Oregon forest. Then they began to farm their land. In 1862, President Lincoln passed the Homestead Act, which said that families that reached Oregon could have 160 acres of land to farm. For the first five years, all they had to do was build a house on the land and live on it and farm it. After five years the land was theirs. On the land, pioneers grew fields of wheat and planted apple orchards.

Wheat field in the Northwest

Pioneers never forgot their experience traveling west. They never forgot how hard and dangerous the journey was. They always remembered their amazing trip across America.

In 1869, the first transcontinental railroad joined the West to the East. No longer were wagon trains rolling across the prairie lands with their wooden wheels. Now, steel wheels sped across the country. They carried people to the West in only a few days compared with the five-month trip it took by wagon. The need for covered wagons slowly disappeared as more people settled the West.

Glossary

49ers: the more than 30,000 people who went west looking for gold in 1849.

California Gold Rush: period of time in 1849 when people rushed to California to dig or pan for gold.

Cascade Mountains: mountain range in western United States that goes through Washington, Oregon, and northern California. It was the last range of mountains the pioneers had to cross when they were headed to Oregon Country.

Cholera: a disease caused by drinking bad water that brings about severe stomach problems.

Cowboys: men or boys who work with cattle on a ranch.

Droppings: dung or animal waste.

Exodusters: freed slaves who moved west (mostly to Kansas, Nebraska, and Oklahoma) in the 1800s to own their own land. They believed they were on an "exodus" or a journey to freedom. Benjamin "Pap" Singleton was the leader of the movement and helped hundreds of freed slaves settle in the West and own their own land.

Gold Fever: an extreme excitement that spread to many people in 1849 to go and search for gold in the West.

Independence Day: July fourth. A national holiday celebrating the signing of the Declaration of Independence in 1776, which said that America was not ruled by England anymore.

Lumberjacks: people whose job is to chop down trees and transport the logs to a sawmill.

Mormon religion: a religion founded by Joseph Smith, Jr. in the 1800s.

Oregon Trail: a 2,000-mile route used by pioneers between 1841 and 1869 to travel over land to the West. The route stretched over present-day Missouri, Kansas, Nebraska, Wyoming, Idaho, and Oregon.

Pioneers: people who were the first to travel to the West in the 1800s.

Plains: large, flat areas of land without trees.

Rocky Mountains: major mountain range of western North America, it splits the United States in two and is part of what is called the Continental Divide. It extends from British Columbia to northern New Mexico. It was one of the ranges the pioneers had to cross in order to get to Oregon Country.

Slaves: people who are owned by someone and made to work hard for no pay.

Sod: the layer of grass and soil that forms the surface of the ground.

Soddies: pioneers who lived on the prairie and whose houses were made of sod.

Spirit of America: popular feeling Americans had in the 1800s that they were able to do things by themselves, without the help of others, and that they could survive in difficult situations and be successful at whatever they chose to do with their lives.

Stampede: a headlong rush of a herd of animals that gallop because they are scared.

Threshing machine: a machine that separates the grain from the stalks and husks of plants by beating the grain in a cylinder with serrated bars that rotate at a high speed. The beating releases the grain from the rest of the plant. The grain can then be crushed and made into flour or used whole.

Wagon train: a long chain of wagons moving together in a line. A popular method of travel used by the pioneers who believed that traveling in large numbers was safer and easier than traveling alone.